I dedicate this book to all classroom teachers,
but especially those who choose early childhood.
You are my heroes and the kindest people I know.
Thank you for letting me be a part of your world.

Susan Salidor

November 2020

D1195864

Sideline Ink Publishing

ISBN: 978-1-7343909-0-2
Ingram Spark Edition

Printed in the United States

Susan Salidor

ONE LITTLE
ACT OF KINDNESS

This book belongs to

- ,

who has the power
to be kind
and the right
to be treated with kindness,
always.

ONE LITTLE ACT OF KINDNESS
CAN GO A LONG, LONG WAY.

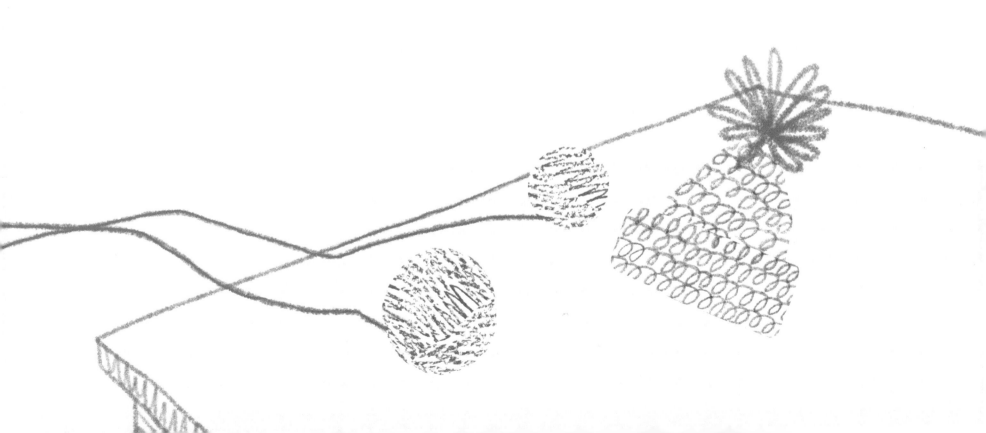

TWO LITTLE ACTS OF KINDNESS
CAN BRIGHTEN ANYONE'S DAY.

THREE LITTLE ACTS OF KINDNESS
CAN MAKE A BEAUTIFUL SOUND.

MANY ACTS OF
KINDNESS

HELP THE WORLD
GO 'ROUND.

ONE LITTLE LOVING WORD
CAN GO A LONG, LONG WAY.

TWO LITTLE LOVING WORDS
CAN BRIGHTEN ANYONE'S DAY.

THREE LITTLE LOVING WORDS
CAN MAKE A BEAUTIFUL SOUND.

Today's Lesson:

ONE LITTLE SEED SOWN
CAN GO A LONG,
LONG WAY.

TWO LITTLE SEEDS SOWN
CAN BRIGHTEN ANYONE'S DAY.

THREE LITTLE SEEDS SOWN
CAN MAKE A BEAUTIFUL SOUND.

OOOOOO!

MANY SEEDS SOWN

ONE LITTLE CHILD'S LAUGHTER
CAN GO A LONG, LONG WAY.

TWO LITTLE CHILDREN'S LAUGHTER CAN BRIGHTEN ANYONE'S DAY.

THREE LITTLE CHILDREN'S LAUGHTER
CAN MAKE A BEAUTIFUL SOUND.

MANY CHILDREN

LAUGHING

HELP THE WORLD
GO 'ROUND.

MANY SEEDS SOWN

HELP THE WORLD GO 'ROUND.

MANY LOVING WORDS

HELP THE WORLD GO 'ROUND.

MANY ACTS OF KINDNESS

HELP THE WORLD GO 'ROUND.

ONE LITTLE ACT OF KINDNESS

Words & Music: Susan Salidor
Arrangement: Valerie Leonhart Smalkin

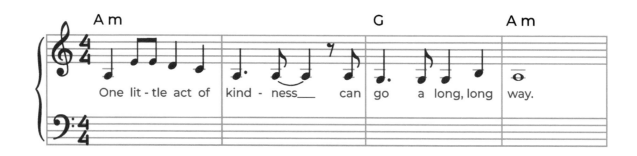

One lit-tle act of kind-ness___ can go a long, long way.

Two lit-tle acts of kind-ness___ can bright-en an-ny-one's___ day.

Three lit-tle acts of kind-ness___ can make a beau-ti-ful___ sound.

Man - y acts of kind - ness ___ help the world go round.

Verse Two
One little loving word can go a long, long way.
Two little loving words can brighten anyone's day.
Three little loving words can make a beautiful sound.
Many loving words help the world go 'round.

Verse Three
One little seed sown can go a long, long way.
Two little seeds sown can brighten anyone's day.
Three little seeds sown can make a beautiful sound.
Many seeds sown help the world go 'round.

Verse Four
One little child's laughter can go a long, long way.
Two little children's laughter can brighten anyone's day.
Three little children's laughter can make a beautiful sound.
Many children laughing help the world go 'round.

And many seeds sown help the world go round.
Many loving words help the world go round,
And many acts of kindness help the world go round.

CPSIA information can be obtained
at www.ICGtesting.com
Printed in the USA
LVHW011458111220
673943LV00006B/114